Austin's Bat Colony
Bristlecone Pines
The Flaming Fountain
Marfa Mystery Lights
Meteor Crater

The Mystery Spot
The Old Man of the Mountain
Sand Mountain
Thurston Lava Tube
Yellowstone Lake Whispers

AMERICA'S TOP 10 CURIOSITIES

By
Jenny Tesar

Published by Blackbirch Press, Inc.
260 Amity Road
Woodbridge, CT 06525

©1998 Blackbirch Press, Inc.
First Edition

Printed in the USA

10 9 8 7 6 5 4 3 2 1

Library of Congress Cataloging-in-Publication Data

Tesar, Jenny E.
  America's top 10 curiosities by Jenny Tesar— 1st ed.
    p. cm.—(America's top 10)
  Includes bibliographical references and index.
  Summary: Describes ten naturally occuring curiosities in the United States, including Acoustic Sand Mountain, Austin's bat colony, bristlecone pine trees, the flaming fountain in Pierre, South Dakota, and the Thurston lava tubes.
    ISBN 1-56711-199-8 (alk. paper)
    1. Science—Miscellanea—Juvenile literature. 2. Curiosities and wonders—United States—Juvenile literature. [1. Landforms. 2. Curiosities and wonders.] I. Title. II. Series.
Q163.T32 1998   97–3610
508.73—dc21   CIP
                                                                     AC

BLACKBIRCH PRESS, INC.
WOODBRIDGE, CONNECTICUT

AMERICA'S TOP

10

CURIOSITIES

NM   OK
                    AR
        TX
        Austin's
        Bat Colony   LA

MEXICO   Gulf of Mexico

Austin's Bat Colony

One of nature's most spectacular sights can be seen in downtown Austin, Texas, on a summer evening. Around sunset, thousands of bats emerge from cracks beneath the Congress Avenue Bridge, which spans Town Lake. Forming as many as 5 long columns, the bats fly off into the night.

Austin's colony is the largest urban bat colony in the world. Up to 1.5 million Mexican free-tail bats live underneath the bridge. The adults weigh about half an ounce and have average wingspans of 12 inches.

The bats arrive in mid-March, after leaving their winter homes in Mexico. In early summer, the females give birth to babies, called "pups." When the pups are 5 weeks old, they learn how to fly and how to navigate using reflected sound—a process called "echolocation." By August, the pups are ready to hunt for food with their mothers. This is the best time to see large groups of bats flying away from the bridge. By early November, as the weather cools, the bats leave Austin and fly to Mexico for the winter.

Bats first began living beneath the Congress Avenue Bridge many years ago. The colony grew rapidly after the bridge was rebuilt in 1980. Some people were frightened when they saw so many bats and wanted the bat colony destroyed. They changed their minds, however, when they learned that Mexican free-tail bats are gentle animals and seldom harm people. In fact, Austin's bats are very helpful. Every night they eat up to 30,000 pounds of mosquitoes and other insects!

Name: Often called "the Congress Avenue Bridge bat colony"

Location: Texas

Size of colony: 250,000 to 1.5 million, depending on the time of year

When the bats are seen: From mid-March to early November. The best time is early evening, especially during July and August.

Fun fact: Mexican free-tail bats travel as far as 800 miles between their summer and winter homes.

Opposite page:
City residents gather to witness the dramatic flight of the bats at sunset.

Bristlecone Pines

★ ★ ★ ★ ★ ★ ★ ★ ★ ★ ★ ★ ★ ★ ★ ★ ★ ★ ★

Bristlecone pines are the oldest trees in the world. Some are 5,000 years old—and still growing! They are found at high altitudes on dry mountains in the American Southwest. Bristlecone pines grow very slowly. One 700-year-old tree studied by scientists was only 3 feet tall and its trunk was only 3 inches wide. To find out the age of a living tree, scientists first drill out a cylinder, or core, of wood. The core is then examined under a microscope to determine the number of annual rings.

There are 2 species, or kinds, of bristlecone pines. The Rocky Mountain bristlecone grows in Colorado and Utah. The Great Basin bristlecone is found mainly in the White and Panamint Mountains of southeastern California. The oldest bristlecone pines are found in the White Mountains. These trees have strange, twisted shapes, and they are dead except for a narrow core of living bark. This bark carries water from the soil up through the trunk. These pines may have just one living branch and only a few twigs that bear needles. The dead wood of a bristlecone pine does not rot easily, however, but remains solid, and supports the tree's living parts.

Young bristlecone pines have green, smooth bark. As the trees age, their bark becomes scaly. Although most pine trees keep their needles for 2 or 3 years, bristlecone pine needles remain on the trees for 12 to 20 years. When they are about 20 years old, these trees begin producing hard, reddish-brown cones. These cones have sharp, bristle-like prickles, for which the trees are named.

Name: For the bristle-like prickles on the pine cones.
Location: American Southwest (California, Arizona, New Mexico, Nevada, Colorado, Utah)
Age: Up to 5,000 years
Height: Usually less than 50 feet
Cones: 1.5 to 3.5 inches long
Fun fact: A bristlecone pine that is no taller than a human may be more than 900 years old.

Opposite page:
The ancient bristlecone pines in the White Mountains are the oldest trees on earth.

AMERICA'S TOP
10
CURIOSITIES

MT
ND
MN
WY
SD ★ Flaming
Fountain
IA
NE

The Flaming Fountain

★ ★ ★ ★ ★ ★ ★ ★ ★ ★ ★ ★ ★ ★

On the grounds of the state capitol in Pierre, South Dakota, is America's most curious fountain. This fountain is created by water that flows from an underground source. The water is burning hot and contains natural gas.

Hot underground water is common in the prairies of South Dakota. Early pioneers discovered that this water could be used for heating. In the early 1900s, engineers drilled a well next to the capitol. The water was used to heat the capitol and other buildings. This method didn't work, however, because chemicals in the water corroded the pipes and other equipment.

In the 1950s, after an explosion occurred in one of the buildings, the heating system was abandoned. Now the hot water runs underground and into Capitol Lake. The water contains so much natural gas that it can be ignited at the point where it comes out of the ground. Once lit, it burns continuously. Today the Flaming Fountain is the center of a memorial honoring veterans of the Korean and Vietnam Wars.

The one problem with the Flaming Fountain is that it smells terrible! The water that bubbles out of the ground contains so much sulfur that people standing near the fountain sometimes get headaches or become nauseated from the fumes. Fortunately, the fumes cannot be smelled from the edge of Capitol Lake. Because most of the lake water comes from the fountain, ice doesn't form unless the temperature falls below 10 degrees Fahrenheit. The area near the fountain never freezes.

Name: Recognizes the ability of the sulfurous water to burn

Location: South Dakota

Temperature of water coming from the ground: 100 to 112 degrees Fahrenheit

Created: In the early 1900s

Fun fact: Natural gas is a fossil fuel. It is formed from the remains of organisms that lived millions of years ago.

Opposite page:
The flaming fountain burns because its water source contains natural gas.

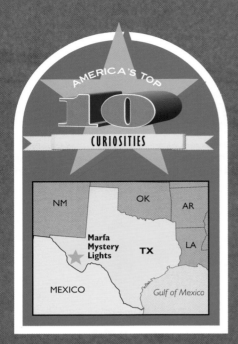

AMERICA'S TOP

10

CURIOSITIES

NM

OK

AR

Marfa
Mystery
Lights

TX

LA

MEXICO

Gulf of Mexico

Marfa Mystery Lights

On many evenings, and in all kinds of weather, strange lights can be seen near the base of the Chianti Mountains in western Texas. They appear soon after sunset and continue until dawn. The lights seem to be suspended in the air. They glow brightly, bounce around, flicker, disappear, and then suddenly reappear. Accounts of the lights vary widely. They have been described as white lights and colored lights, as single lights and clusters of lights. Some people say that the lights look like small balls of fire while others say they are as big as basketballs. The lights have been said to glow softly and to dance like candle flames.

The lights are always viewed from the same site—about 10 miles east of the small town of Marfa. No one, however, can identify the source or location of the lights. In fact, the lights disappear or move out of reach whenever they are approached.

No one knows how long the mystery lights have been appearing. The Apaches saw them in the 1800s and maybe even earlier. In 1883, a man named Robert Ellison reported seeing the lights, and since then, thousands of people have also viewed them. The lights have even become a popular tourist attraction.

Although no one knows why the lights appear, many explanations have been proposed. The Apaches believed the lights to be falling stars. Others have suggested that lightning or other atmospheric phenomena are the cause. Stranger explanations include glow-in-the-dark rabbits, the ghosts of dead lovers, and visitors from outer space.

Name: Honors Marfa, a town about 10 miles west of the lights
Location: Texas
When the lights are seen: Between sunset and midnight
Discovered: Probably in the early 1800s
Fun fact: The town of Marfa was named by an engineer's wife for the heroine in a Russian novel.

Opposite page:
These lights, which have been witnessed for hundreds of years, have never been explained.

AMERICA'S TOP
10
CURIOSITIES

NV   UT   CO

CA   **Meteor
Crater** ★

AZ   NM

MEXICO

Meteor Crater

About 50,000 years ago, an object from outer-space crashed into the earth, blasting a hole in the middle of the Arizona desert. Scientists call this hole the Barringer Meteorite Crater after the engineer who first proposed that it was produced by a meteorite. (Any object that travels through the earth's atmosphere and hits the ground is called a meteorite.) Most people simply call the hole Meteor Crater.

The meteorite that created the crater was an asteroid—a small, planet-like object that orbits the sun. Because asteroids travel very fast, they do not have to be large to cause a lot of damage. The asteroid that created Meteor Crater is believed to have been about 150 feet in diameter and traveling at approximately 40,000 miles per hour when it hit the ground. The collision destroyed most of the asteroid, leaving only small fragments. These tiny pieces show that the object from space was made mostly of iron and nickel.

The crater looks like a giant bowl. It is 560 feet deep and 4,180 feet across. Its rim rises 160 feet above the surrounding plain. This hole is big enough to hold 20 football fields, and could seat 2 million people on its sloping sides!

Meteor Crater played a role in America's Apollo Space Program, which sent men to the moon. Apollo astronauts were trained in Meteor Crater to learn about the geology of craters caused by asteroids.

Name: Honors mining engineer Daniel Moreau Barringer
Location: Arizona
Depth: 560 feet
Width: 4,180 feet
Discovered: Originally by Native Americans (date unknown); first written report in 1871
Fun fact: Meteor Crater is deep enough to contain the Washington Monument.

Opposite page:
Meteor Crater is the earth's largest, best-preserved crater made by an asteroid.

AMERICA'S TOP

10

CURIOSITIES

OR   ID

CA

NV

UT

Mystery
Spot

Pacific Ocean

AZ

MEXICO

The
Mystery Spot

★ ★ ★ ★ ★ ★ ★ ★ ★ ★ ★ ★ ★ ★ ★ ★

The force of gravity pulls objects toward the center of the earth. Because of gravity, people stand perpendicular to the ground and not at an angle. Gravity also causes balls to roll downhill rather than uphill. At the Mystery Spot, near Santa Cruz, California, however, objects roll uphill and people appear to lean backwards or sideways. Even the trees do not grow perpendicular to the ground!

Have the laws of gravity gone haywire at the Mystery Spot? Different theories have been proposed to explain the phenomenon there, but so far none have been proven. The most widely believed explanation is that there are magnetic rocks beneath the ground—perhaps remains of a meteorite—that interfere with the force of gravity and cause it to pull at an unusual angle.

Walking through the Mystery Spot is an eerie experience. People must lean to maintain their balance, and when walking uphill, they must climb straight-legged.

One popular demonstration at the Mystery Spot shows the strange forces at work there. Two bricks are placed on the ground and are shown to be level with each other. When 2 people of equal height stand on the bricks, 1 person appears to be taller. When they switch places, however, the person who appeared taller now looks several inches shorter!

Even airplanes flying overhead are affected by the strange forces at the Mystery Spot. Their compasses sometimes swing as much as 40 degrees off course!

Name: Recognizes that the cause of this curiosity is still a mystery
Location: California
Size of area: About 150 feet in diameter
Discovered: 1940
Fun fact: Some people say they get headaches or upset stomachs in the Mystery Spot. Other people say they feel better there than they do anywhere else!

Opposite page:
An official guide at the Mystery Spot shows one of the strange effects there. The guide is not intentionally leaning, nor does he fall over.

AMERICA'S TOP

10

CURIOSITIES

CANADA

ME

VT

Old Man
of the
Mountain

NY

NH

Atlantic
Ocean

MA

The
Old Man of the Mountain

The official symbol of the state of New Hampshire is the 40-foot-high rock face of the Old Man of the Mountain. It is formed from 6 huge granite slabs that jut out from a cliff in the shape of a man's profile. The Old Man of the Mountain was first discovered by the Abenaki tribe. Later, in 1805, Francis Whitcomb and Luke Brooks noticed the profile while working on a road through Franconia Notch—a narrow pass in the White Mountains. They thought it looked like Thomas Jefferson, who was president of the United States at the time.

The Old Man of the Mountain was carved by nature. About 50,000 years ago, a large glacier, or sheet of ice, moved through Franconia Notch. It removed huge amounts of soil and rock from the mountain, leaving behind the rough outlines of a face. The finer details were carved by a combination of freezing and thawing.

To help protect the Old Man's profile, some of the rocks have been braced with cables and anchor irons. Cracks are sealed with a tough substance called epoxy. Aqueducts made of stone and cement have been built on top of the mountain to direct water away from the face.

The Old Man of the Mountain is best viewed from the shore of Profile Lake. This lake is 1,200 feet below the Old Man, at the base of Cannon Mountain. Millions of people have come here to see and photograph the granite profile. Many have read Nathaniel Hawthorne's story, called *The Great Stone Face*, which was inspired by this natural curiosity.

Name: Based on a story by Nathaniel Hawthorne
Location: New Hampshire
Height of face: 40 feet
Discovered: Originally, by the Abenaki tribe (date unknown); later 2 surveyors, Francis Whitcomb and Luke Brooks, in 1805.
Fun fact: Cannon Mountain is named for a horizontal rock that juts out from the mountainside and looks like the barrel of a cannon.

Opposite page:
The striking granite features of the Old Man were carved entirely by natural forces.

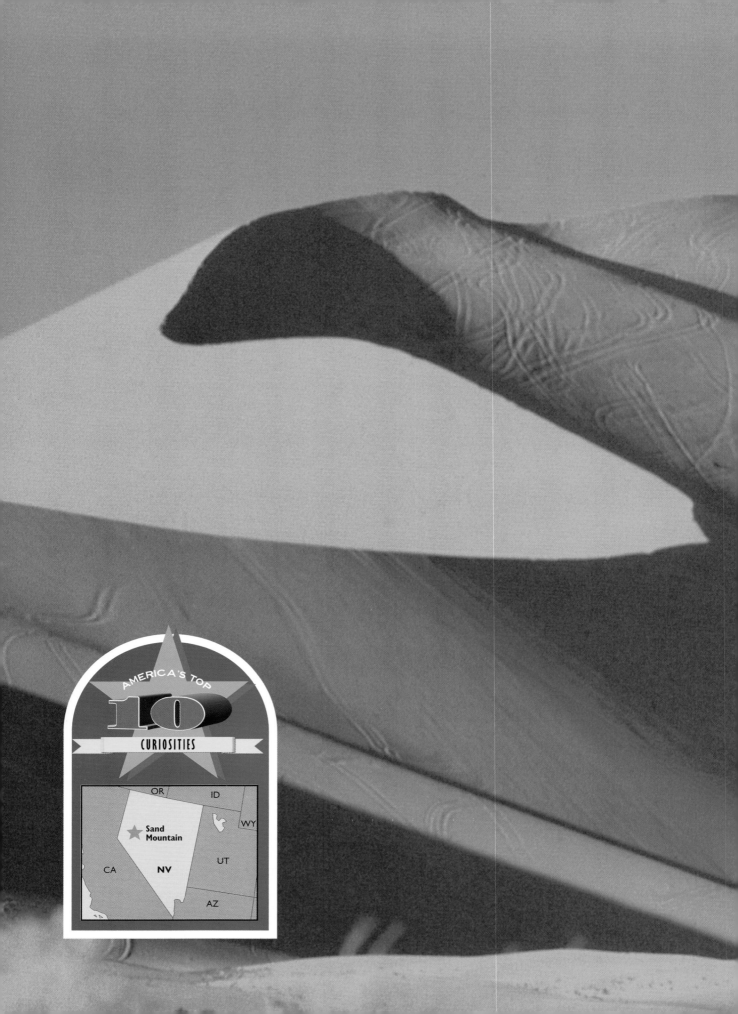

AMERICA'S TOP

10

CURIOSITIES

OR | ID
WY
★ Sand
Mountain
CA | NV | UT
AZ

Sand Mountain

The stretch of U.S. Highway 50 that crosses Nevada is known as "the loneliest highway in America." It passes dry sagebrush, deserted mining towns, and a hill that makes strange noises. This hill, called Sand Mountain, is in western Nevada, about 25 miles southeast of the town of Fallon. The "mountain," known as "seif" dune for its long, sword-like shape, is actually a sand dune about 600 feet high and 2.5 miles long.

Walk up Sand Mountain, and you'll hear all kinds of noises that sound like moans, booms, and loud roars. These sounds come from beneath your feet. Some of them are so loud that they can be heard up to 7 miles away!

The sounds occur when the sand moves—for example, when people walk over it, animals run across it, or wind pushes it around. The rubbing together of the sand particles produces the sounds.

The musical sands of Sand Mountain are a natural curiosity, but they are not unique. There are musical sands in other parts of the world. Scientists have discovered two kinds of musical sands. Dry and highly polished sand particles—such as those that make up Sand Mountain—produce low, booming sounds. Particles that are large and almost perfectly round produce high, squeaky sounds.

No one knows when Sand Mountain was first discovered. It was probably known to Native Americans who lived in the area centuries ago. Early pioneers who travelled through the area probably heard the musical sounds, along with riders on the Pony Express.

Name: Known as "seif" dune, after the Arabic word "sayf," meaning sword.
Location: Nevada
Size: About 600 feet high and 2.5 miles long
Discovered: Date unknown. The first written description was in 1883.
Fun fact: One of the residents of Sand Mountain is the Sand Mountain blue butterfly, which feeds on buckwheat.

Opposite page:
Some of the strange sounds made on Sand Mountain can be heard up to 7 miles away.

Thurston
Lava Tube

HI

Thurston Lava Tube

On Hawaii's Big Island lies an ancient tunnel. It's about 450 feet long—about 90 feet longer than a football field—with a ceiling at least 10 feet high. In some places, the tunnel is as wide as a living room. This tunnel is the Thurston Lava Tube, also known by its Hawaiian name, Nahuku. It was formed during an eruption of the volcano Kilavea that created the Big Island.

Far below the earth's crust are areas of hot, molten (liquid) rock. This molten rock comes to the surface through cracks in the crust. At the surface, it is called "lava." Sometimes lava shoots out in violent eruptions. The Hawaiian Islands were formed mainly by a series of quiet eruptions. The lava poured out from openings in the tops and sides of the volcanoes and flowed downhill toward the sea. This process is still taking place on the Big Island today.

Lava from the Big Island's erupting volcanoes flows in two ways: It either spreads out in puddles or runs in streams through narrow channels. Lava tubes are formed by several processes. Sometimes the lava on the surface of a lava stream cools and hardens, while the lava below the hardened surface remains molten and continues to flow—just as water flows through a pipe. When the eruption ends, or the lava finds another path, the molten lava drains out, leaving a hardened tunnel, or lava tube.

Close examination of the interior of the Thurston Lava Tube shows how it was shaped by various flows. The marks on the walls indicate how the lava stream eroded the ground.

Name: Honors publisher Lorrin A. Thurston, who began an effort to make the lava tube and its surroundings a public park. Nahuku, its Hawaiian name, means "the protuberances."
Location: Hawaii
Length: About 450 feet
Height: 6–12 feet
Fun fact: Lava tubes usually are widest and deepest near the vent of a volcano. They become narrower and more shallow farther away.

Opposite page:
Lava tubes can be as large as a whole house.

MT

★ Yellowstone
Lake Whispers

ID   SD

WY

NE

UT   CO

Yellowstone Lake Whispers

Can a lake talk? Long ago, Native Americans heard whispering sounds near the Yellowstone and Shoshone Lakes in Wyoming. They believed that spirits were talking near the lakes. In the 1800s, fur trappers also heard the lakes "talking." In 1872, a man named F. Bradley described the phenomenon as "a hoarse whine." Then in 1893, Edwin Linton wrote about "a strange echoing sound in the sky." Other people have compared the sounds to bells, harps, humming bees, and rushing wind.

No one knows what produces the sounds. The most likely cause might be wind blowing across the lakes or over the surrounding mountains. But there is no evidence of wind when the sounds are heard. Leaves on the trees do not move, nor are ripples seen on the lakes.

Another theory suggests that the sounds originate far below the earth's surface, where there is molten, or hot liquid, rock. This liquid rock heats water under the ground in the Yellowstone region that eventually comes to the surface in the form of hot springs, such as geysers. Heat escapes from the water when it reaches the earth's surface, and this may produce the whispering sounds. These sounds are heard only near the two lakes, however, and never near the geysers.

Because the sounds are soft and usually do not last longer than half a minute, they are difficult to hear. They are most often heard early in the morning in a quiet area. The sounds are rarely heard in the summer, when the park is filled with tourists.

Name: Describes the soft sounds heard near Yellowstone Lake and Shoshone Lake

Location: Wyoming

Discovered: By Native Americans (date unknown)

Fun fact: In the middle of winter, when Yellowstone Lake is covered with thick ice, some spots on the lake bottom are near boiling point.

Opposite page:
No one knows what produces the whispering sounds around the Yellowstone and Shoshone lake region.

The 10 curiosities in this book are all naturally occurring phenomena. They were chosen for a number of different reasons, such as uniqueness, age, size, geological interest, and mysterious quality. Below is a list of more curiosities.

More American Curiosities

| Name, Location, *Description* |

Alaskan Peninsula, Alaska. *Longest peninsula.*

Bagley Icefields, Alaska. *Largest icefield.*

Big Room at Carlsbad, New Mexico. *Largest cave room.*

Cape Disappointment, Washington. *Foggiest place.*

Columbia Glacier, Alaska. *Fastest moving glacier.*

Crater Lake, Oregon. *Deepest lake.*

Death Valley, California. *Lowest spot.*

El Capitan, California. *Largest block of granite.*

Everglades, Florida. *Largest marsh.*

Grand Canyon, Arizona. *Largest gorge.*

Great Salt Lake, Utah. *Largest inland body of salt water.*

Lachuguilla Cave, New Mexico. *Deepest cave.*

Lake Michigan, Illinois, Indiana, Michigan, Wisconsin. *Largest lake.*

Landscape Arch, Utah. *Longest natural arch.*

Lost Sea, Tennessee. *Largest underground lake.*

Mammoth Cave National Park, Kentucky. *Most extensive cave system.*

Mauna Loa, Hawaii. *Largest active volcano.*

Mississippi River, Minnesota, Wisconsin, Iowa, Illinois, Missouri, Kentucky, Tennessee, Arkansas, Mississippi, Louisiana. *Longest river.*

Mississippi River delta, Louisiana. *Largest delta.*

Mojave Desert, California. *Largest desert.*

Molokai sea cliffs, Hawaii. *Highest sea cliffs.*

Mount McKinley, Alaska. *Highest mountain.*

Mount Waialeale, Hawaii. *Wettest place.*

New River, West Virginia. *Deepest river.*

North Fork Roe River, Montana. *Shortest named river.*

Ribbon Falls, California. *Highest continuous waterfall.*

Sea Lion Cave, Oregon. *Largest sea cave.*

Steamboat Geyser, Wyoming. *Tallest active geyser.*

Yellowstone, Montana, Wyoming. *Largest geothermal basin.*

Glossary

annual ring The annual growth of a tree.

asteroid A small planet-like object that travels around the sun.

colony A group of similar organisms that live in a particular area.

crater A bowl-shaped hole in the ground formed by a meteorite, volcano, or geyser.

echolocation The ability to use reflected sounds for navigation.

glacier A large sheet of ice.

granite A hard rock made of quartz and other minerals.

gravity The force of attraction that pulls objects toward the center of the earth.

lava Molten rock.

meteorite An object that travels through the earth's atmosphere and hits the ground.

notch A deep, narrow pass through a mountain range.

theory A possible—but unproven—answer to a question.

Further Reading

Bolt, Bruce A. *Discover Volcanoes and Earthquakes.* Lake Forest, IL: Forest House, 1992.

Brewer, Duncan. *Comets, Asteroids and Meteorites.* Tarrytown, NY: Marshall Cavendish, 1992.

Butler, Daphne. *What Happens When Volcanoes Erupt?* Chatham, NJ: Raintree Steck-Vaughn, 1995.

Carlisle, Madelyn. *Let's Investigate Magical, Mysterious Meteorites.* Hauppauge, NY: Barron's Educational Series, 1992.

Lauber, Patricia. *Voyagers from Space: Meteors and Meteorites.* New York: HarperCollins Children's Books, 1989.

Where to Get On-Line Information

To learn more about the fascinating world of bats, visit the web site for Bat Conservation International, Inc., at http://www.batcon.org

Visit the Bristlecone Pines website at http://www.sonic.net/bristlecone/intro.html

Visit Meteor Crater Enterprises, Inc., at http://www.flagstaff.az.us/meteor

To view some of the unusual phenomena at the Mystery Spot, visit their web page at http://www.mystery-spot.com

For a closer look at Hawaii's volcanoes, visit Hawaii Volcanoes National Park at http://www.book.uci.edu/Books/Moon/volcanoes.html

To learn more about Yellowstone National Park, visit the park's web site at http://www.nps.gov/yell

Index

Photo Credits